EUODIA: APOSTOLIC TRAILBLAZER

(Paul's conflict resolution/reconciliation ministry)

Dr. Cynthia King Bolden-Gardner, J.D.,D.Div.

TABLE OF CONTENTS

Dedication i
Comments from Colleagues ii
INTRODUCTION: Journey Outline 1
CHAPTER 1: Backdrop: History and Historical Significance of Philippi 6
CHAPTER 2: The Case for Apostleship 9
CHAPTER 3: Christian Family Feud: Euodia and Syntyche (What's it Really all About?) 15
CHAPTER 4: satan, The Genesis of Strife 25
CHAPTER 5: Me Too?! Laying The Blame at God's Feet ... 31
CHAPTER 6: *STRIFE* Devours Tribes. Here's the Solution. ... 37
CHAPTER 7: Moving Toward a Unified House 42
CHAPTER 8: Koinonia: Unified on the Mount of God 49

Closing Prayer 54
Inspirational Bibliography 56
Other Books by the Author 58
About The Author 60

DEDICATION

To my Beloved Bigma, the late Missionary Lela Mae James, and Apostle Mom, the late Apostle Dr. Annie B. Campbell-Pitre.

&

All of our Apostolic sisters (and 'sympatico' brethren) who earnestly CONTEND for the faith. This is in celebration of WOMEN this month and year---a long-awaited honor and past due debt of love. Praise God for the power to overcome historical Biblically-enforced sexism and current, but receding, societal opposition to WOMEN as fivefold clerics.

Thank Jehovah Tsidkenu for exousia, dunamis, kratos, thronos to confront the fretting contentiousness of our female colleagues. Ladies, we are SISTERS mandated to JOIN HEARTS AND HANDS to scale and conquer the Seven Mountains.

Philippians 4:1-4 KJV:

Therefore, my brethren dearly beloved and longed for, my joy and my crown, so stand fast in the Lord my dearly beloved. I beseech Euodias and beseech Syntyche that they be of the same mind in the Lord.

And I entreat you also, true yokefellow, help those women which labored with me in the Gospel, with Clement also, and with other my fellow-laborers whose names are in the Book of Life.

Rejoice in the Lord always, and again I say rejoice.

NOTE: satan will always be lowercase as a matter of this author's choice.

COMMENTS FROM COLLEAGUES

Will the real anointed and strong Women of God, please stand! Yes, you! 2019 is your year to stand out and be counted as the one who will cry aloud and spare not, lift up your voice like a trumpet…..(Isaiah 58:1) KJV. For you Apostle Cynthia Bolden-Gardner, have been chosen for such a time as this. So, keep speaking and teaching the Word of God, keep praying, keep believing, keep shining and most of all, keep Living Your God-designed life on purpose and you will receive your Crown of Life in the end. May God continue to bless you for all the lives that you have touched.

I am so honored to be a part of your life.

Evangelist Ella Vaught-Gardner

Apostle Cynthia Gardner and I grew up together. She is a riveting and dynamic communicator who ignites her audiences with passion and truth for women. Her encouragement propels other into their purpose and destiny beyond mediocrity and complacency. Rebuilding the lives of those who have been wounded through stereotypes and generalizations regarding their identity.

Apostle DAVID Paul Purdue
Sage Communications
Macon, Georgia

A leader in her own right as a Female Apostle, Apostle CKB Gardner, through this subject matter is adding yet again to the body of knowledge necessary to strengthen the priesthood and all genders of the called. And so is it that through this work Apostle Cynthia King-Bolden-Gardner shall be known as "The repairer of the breach, the restorer of paths to dwell in" Crying loud and sparing not for the cause of Christ and the greater good for the body. The fast has been called, the Lord has heard, the wicked shall cease, and righteousness shall speak.

Elder Dr. Carmen Vaughn-Hewitt, D.Min.
Outreach Site Pastor from St Stephens Baptist Church, Temple Hills, Md.

I met Apostle Gardner last December after months of collaborating in the gospel online.

I saw the glory of God in her and her remarkable passion for the people and Kingdom of God. She is like the Prophet Jeremiah interceding and weeping for the people constantly in the presence of Almighty God.

She is gifted, anointed and unwavering in her commitment to reach the globe with the gospel.

This book will be a blessing and a definite inspiration to others.

Apostle John Stephan
Full Gospel Baptist Fellowship of Gurdaspur
Punjab, India

INTRODUCTION:
Journey Outline

Thank you for agreeing to join in this incredible journey.

Three months ago, right after Thanksgiving, I was awakened out of a good snoring session at 3 A.M. I saw the word Euodia suspended in the air as though written on a blank wall. Try as I might, curiosity got the best of me and I could not return to sleep. Sleep is such a precious commodity!

I began flipping Bibles, research aids listed in the back of this book, the Internet, and anywhere or anything else I could find. Who is she and what is she to me?

As I continued to research, I found that her name was actually found in Philippians 4 (all Scripture references are KJV unless otherwise indicated). Further excavating revealed that her name was spelled Euodias, definitely masculine, and historically, she was decidedly male!

PHILIPPIANS 4:1-2 KJV

Therefore, my brethren dearly beloved and longed for, my joy and crown, so stand fast in the Lord, my dearly beloved.

I beseech Euodia and Syntyche, that they be of the same mind in the Lord.

Further inquiry led to *'pay dirt'*. Euodia is a woman along with Syntyche. She is not a man as originally projected and as she has continued to be portrayed for centuries in Scripture. *Euodia* means *'sweet fragrance'* or *'prosperous journey'*.

The name *Euodia* reflects a tropical plant now known as *Tetradium danielli,* with shiny, dark, glossy leaves and a bark that resembles a birch or ash tree, with tiny, white, summer flowers that are highly attractive to honey bees.

The name encompasses that which is deep, rich, pure. *Sweet fragrance* is of the highest order, inferring a sweet-smelling savor or sacrifice unto the Lord.

Tetra signifies four, like the men that carried the paralytic and tore the roof off to lower him before Jesus. The number four speaks of unity, compassion, and cooperation. E.W. Bullinger, Number in Scripture (Kregel Publication 1864, 1967).

Looking at her name, Euodia may have been petite, delicate, and dark, but reflecting an aura of purity and innocence at the time of her birth, like the description of the little white blossoms. Whoever named her doted upon her and looked upon her as a dainty, fragrant flower. All of this denotes tenderness, someone truly cherished. Strong's Greek Concordance 2136 states Euodia was derived from *'euodoo'* which means *'fine traveling, not inconsistent with the prosperous journey'*.

Syntyche stands for 'fortunate' or 'fate'. *Syntyche* or *Syntyka* or *Syntyche* in Strong's Concordance 4941 is derived from *'suntugchano'* denoting *'an accident'*. Inferentially, her name appears to be the more secular or idolatrous in of the two. Presumably, her family was more attuned to the belief in pagan gods, fate, fortune, and the worship and sacrifices attendant to the same. This idolatrous worship is set forth in the next Historical chapter in detail. Whatever their true personalities and background, it speaks volumes that they were actually female Christian converts.

The name of Clement, the presumed messenger (other than Epaphroditus) of Paul sent beseeching them to be at peace, means *'mild, merciful, lenient and compassionate'*, all of which suit one on this holy peacemaking errand.

The *Apostolic Constitutions*, which were allegedly written in 4th Century A.D. by the Twelve Apostles, originating in Syria, contends for Euodia being a male. Enter Paul with the women who assisted him in the Gospel including the feuding Euodias, misspelled like Junias, both presumed to be males, and Syntyche, Euodia's cross (pun intended) counterpart. It was speculated that Euodias and Syntyche were dueling spouses of the church at Philippi. This speculation of mere matrimonial discord has proven to be in error. *Wikipedia, "Apostolic Constitutions" (Global), 2014.*

Like Junia(s), who was for centuries initially presumptively male because of phobic changes in the text, these women are highly likely to be Apostles. *Highly likely* because they were part of the apostolic group led by Paul.

Euodia and Syntyche are not unlike those in the church in the house of Phoebe (Romans 16 KJV), Priscilla, Aquilla, Mary, Andronicus, Junia, Amphlias, Urbane, Stachys, Apelles, Aristobulos, Narcissus, Tryphena, Tryphosa, Persis, Rufus, Asyncritus, Phlegon, Hermas, Patrobas, Hermes, Philololugus, Julia, Nereus, and Olympus.

Paul urged Euodia and Syntyche to 'agree in the Lord' indicating that this was no minuscule matter of marital discord and counseling. *Henry, Matthew (1960) [1710/1811] "Philippians". In Church, Leslie (Ed.) Matthew Henry's Commentary on the Whole Bible (Broad Oak Ed.) Marshall, Morgan and Scott, Ltd.* "Euodias and Syntyche it seems were at variance, either one with the other or with the church."

At the time of his writing to Euodia and Syntyche, Paul was incarcerated for casting demons out of a divining woman (Acts 16:16-24 KJV). In so doing, he caused great financial loss to her slave owners and threatened the reigning 'religious' order.

This writing in conjunction with his incarceration have led some to speculate that Euodias, the alleged male, was a *'goaler'*, a jailer, a prison guard (Acts 16:25-34 KJV). He is supposedly the very one who was saved after the 'earthquake' that really freed Paul and Silas, who did not seize the opportunity to escape. *"Euodia", Bible Study Tools/ International Standard Encyclopedia 12/6/2017.*

Whatever stance you take on their Apostleship, Dear Reader, if you are a woman, the objective is to instill a healthy sense of self-worth, especially if you are in the ministry.

Second, this is being written to help celebrate 2019, which has been deemed 'The Year of the Woman' by many, including such giants in the prophetic and apostolic lecturing circles as James W. Goll, Cindy Jacobs, and Steve Schultz of Elijah List.

We see many women accelerating to positions as CEOs, entrepreneurs, heads of banks, law firms, founders of nondenominational ministries, denominational Bishops, film directors, Grammy and Oscar winners, leaders in IT and AI after years of excelling without recognition. Due to the exertion of these women and the unblemished character they have maintained, the doors have been flung wide open for others to follow.

Next, because there was an issue between these two women (I beseech Euodia and Syntyche to be of the same mind), the source of which is speculated, an examination of the issue of strife, internecine warfare, and how Paul 'puts it to bed' is discussed. Paul, the statesman, is a skilled resolver of conflict and a reconciler. A comparison is made with how Paul tenderly and diplomatically addresses the issue between Euodia and Syntyche and his caustic dealings with reprobates Hymaneus, Philetus, Hermogenes, and Alexander.

Prior to delving into these Pauline peacemaking efforts, a quick glance at division in the Garden of Eden, the genesis of strife, is reviewed.

Why deal with strife at all, one might ask. Strife has been the number one hindrance to the promotion and fulfillment of destiny and purpose for women. Men have had their part in it; but do not bare all of the blame. Women have been undermining and cutting one another's throats 'from time immemorial'. One need only look at Sarai and Hagar, Hannah and Peninah, Leah and Rachel…the Bible has a plethora of examples. See, Kingdom Seed, Book I, Woman, Know Thyself! (Xlibris 2011) by Bishop Cynthia King Bolden Gardner.

In closing, we take a look at unity, koinonia, what it means to the body of Christ and our final destination, the Mount of God, one flesh as His Bride.

We close with a prayer.

CHAPTER 1

Backdrop: History and Historical Significance of Philippi

In order to fully understand these women, Euodia and Syntyche, it will be extremely helpful to know the environment in which this ministry is planted.

Philippi, where these women are and to which Paul addresses the missile, was colonized by the Romans but mimicked Greek culture. The area was relatively wealthy with gold and silver mines. It grew as swamps were drained and used for local agriculture.

Women were not completely equal with the men, but were cherished and provided for by parents, spouses, and male siblings in a culture where goddesses, sexual fetishes, and excesses abounded in the form of offerings and ritual sacrifices. *Archeological Study Bible*, Zondervan (2010).

Philippi only had a few Jewish converts and they lacked a synagogue, so they met near the Krenides River. It was crucial as a city in Eastern Macedon and thrived during the Hellenistic, Roman, and Byzantine periods. Most of the early churches constructed in Philippi were Byzantine. As set forth hereinbelow, women were Paul's primary supporters, including Lydia from Thyatira, the seller of purple. Paul resided at her home.

Philippi was turned into a Roman colony and a military outpost. The citizens of Philippi were accorded the same rights as Romans. There were not enough of them to establish a synagogue.

As Roman colonists, these women enjoyed a level of freedom and independence not common in most Greek cities. Hence the church at Phoebe's, Chloe's and all of the helpers and female Deacons and Apostles discussed below.

As aptly stated by *Lightfoot*:

> They had labored in the gospel and in the honorable company. That is the testimony that is borne of them. The influence of women seems to have been a feature of the Macedonian churches. At Thessalonica it is said "Of the chief women not a few."
> At Berea; "Many of them believed, also of the Greek women of honorable rank not a few." And in connection with the start of the
> Philippian church, it is said, "We spake to the women that were gathered together." "The extant Macedonian inscriptions says Lightfoot, seems to assign to the sex a higher social influence than is common among the civilized nations of antiquity…"

The Pulpit Commentary, Volume 20, The Epistle to the Philippians, at page 175; MacDonald Publishing.

Historically, Philippi was also important as the site of two battles fought in an effort to oust Julius Caesar. The insurrectionists were Cassius and Brutus, in approximately 42 B.C. It was thereafter that Philippi became a 700 square foot Roman colony. Was this same warlike, divisive spirit lingering and mutating in the area and attempting to penetrate and thwart the Gospel in the dispute between Euodia and Syntyche?

There were many impressive buildings in the area, including an arena, Paul's jail, and Byzantine churches all along the Ignatian way. They were destroyed by earthquakes. The Ignatian way was Paul's route between Thessalonica, Apopolis, Philippi, Neapolis, and Apollonia. It was also the route utilized by the Roman soldiers.

Remember, it was one such earthquake recounted in the Bible that shook the jails open. The end result: Paul and Silas were able to save the soul of the guard.

Paul was incarcerated for casting demons out of a divining woman. Acts 16:16-24 KJV. In so doing, he caused great financial loss to her slave owners and threatened the reigning 'religious' order. Ironically, Paul and his companions' Gospel violated Cicero's ordinance against worshipping strange gods. Imagine, strange GOD?

No wonder Paul wrote about their building altars to an UNKNOWN God. Therefore, Paul and Silas were the catalysts of spiritual earthquakes comparable to the physical earthquakes endemic to the area. Acts 16:25-34 KJV. The saturation of his ministry with women, like that of Jesus, added to the 'quaking,' then and now.

CHAPTER 2

THE CASE FOR APOSTLESHIP

It is argued here that the very same misogyny that led to the change of Junia's name to Junias, Euodia's name to Euodias, and that pigeonholed the others as deacons, servants, members, or helpers, is the same sexist and errant spirit that failed to recognize Euodia and perhaps Syntyche as Apostles. I say *perhaps* Syntyche because Paul seems to address the eldest or most responsible and accountable first. Parents do the same. This is not to disparage deacons or any other calling. All are servants, all are Christ's and Christ is God's. As we proceed, we are going to take a look at several of these women in their various capacities, as well as some unnamed Apostles.

Euodia and Syntyche were very much involved in the founding of the church at Philippi. These same women were part of Paul's apostolic ministry along with those in Roman's 16: Julia, who was Rufus' mother and Paul's 'adopted church mother' (Romans 16:13 KJV), Priscilla, wife of Aquilla, Phoebe, Mary, Tryphena, Tryphosa, Persis. All of these women are ministering Roman citizens like Euodia and Syntyche.

Phoebe was called a servant of the church in Cenchrea. It has been construed as deacon or deaconess. Yet, there was a church *formed or founded* at her house. Was that appellation her true calling? Ellicott's Commentary for English readers; *Exposition, The Epistle to the Phlippians, The Pulpit Commentary, Vol. 20, MacDonald Publishing Company*. We still have a contingent today who say women cannot even operate in the capacity of Deacons in the body though others have ordained them! A house divided, indeed. God is not the author of confusion. Man and satan are over that department (I Cor. 14:30 KJV).

Priscilla and Aquila have a church at their house as well, are Paul's helpers in Christ, and have laid down their lives. They are Apostles.

Andronicus and Junia are referred to as Paul's kinsmen and fellow prisoners (yokefellows?) who are of note among the Apostles and were *in Christ before Paul (Romans 16:7 KJV)*.

Is it a mere coincidence that only two women, Junia and Euodia, both admittedly strong and integral to Paul's ministry, were 'buried as males?' If Euodia was of no consequence and simply a member or a deacon, why go to such extremes to obfuscate her sex?

Moreover, why would Paul expend crucial precious prison time and resources to personally address them? As unruly members or deacons, he who had the power to appoint also has the power to disappoint and wash his hands of the ordeal. He did not do so here. As stated hereinbelow, Paul took the ax to Hermogenes, Hymaneus, Philetus, and Alexander…but did not do so with Euodia and Syntyche.

Moreover, in serially looking at documented Apostolic characteristics, School of the Apostles pp.74-76 by Melvin Thompson,

III (2017), Euodia's engagement in the founding of the church at Philippi would definitely constitute *pioneering (Romans 15:20 KJV)* as can be inferred from Strong's defining her as a 'fine traveler.' She was engaged in the Apostolic work of *building (I Corinthians 3:10 KJV), laying a foundation* and *organizing*. It should not be inferred that Apostle Thompson was consulted or has taken a position on this issue. Also, see, generally, ABC's of Apostleship, pp. 20, 78, 165, by Paula A. Price, PhD., PPM Global Resources, Inc. (2015).

Although seemingly uncommendable here, Euodia is indeed engaged in *warring* (2 Corinthians 10:3-5 KJV) with Syntyche, either over the issues of law versus grace, or sincerity of motivation for teaching and preaching the Word. Each of them felt justified in wrangling with the other in pulling down perceived strongholds that they believed contrary to the Word of God (Ibid, School of the Apostles, pp.74-76).

Authority and power (Matthew 10:1; Luke 9:2 KJV) are without question. These are ladies in positions of eminence, leadership within the body engaged in *teaching, preaching, therefore discipling and establishing and advancing the Gospel with boldness.* Each *defending* their respective position and apparently refusing to back down. (Romans 12:7; I Corinthians 2:4; Matthew 28:19-20; Matthew 11:12; 2 Peter 1:12; Jude 1:3; Proverbs 28:1 KJV). School of the Apostles at pp.74-76; see, generally, The Fivefold Ministry Offices, pp.47-51, Paula A. Price, Ph.D. (1994).

The prospects of members or deacons carrying this level of clout and drawing Paul into the resolution of it is improbable. The Philippian church had a Pastor, yet this went higher up the food chain for mediation, to Apostle Paul.

We don't have the 'whole' story on a lot of matters. For example, there are two nameless Apostles referenced by Paul. Historically, with few exceptions, women's names have been omitted from the Bible altogether. Even the names of Christ's sisters have been omitted, although his brothers are listed (Matthew 13:55-56 KJV).

Are these two unspecified Apostles women? Were they the women cautioned to stop yelling across the church? Were they Euodia and Syntyche engaged in mission work?

In 2 Corinthians 8:18 KJV there is a nameless Apostle whose work in the Gospel is praised throughout the church. Further down in verse 22, a nameless Apostle is commended for being diligent in many things. In verse 23, reference is made to messengers of the churches and the glory of Christ, once again, unnamed. All of the Apostles of the Bible, Herbert Lockyer, Zondervan Publishing (1972) on page 243.

As a final postscript, it might be added that while this was already with the publisher, another 'clue' came in the form of the name 'Polycarp.' This brain teaser came at midnight before Good Friday in the midst of fasting. Fascinated once again, the search for truth was resurrected.

Polycarp was a high church dignitary, a reputed Bishop of sorts. More importantly, Polycarp was a contemporary of Clement, who Paul addressed in Phillipians 4 with Euodia and Syntyche. He was a contemporary of Paul, John, and Ignatius and resided in Philippi!

Further research led to a note listing saints and martyrs, contemporaries of these men. There are approximately twenty. One on the list was an Eudokia. She was scribed by some as a martyr of Heliopolis, the sun city in the vicinity of Egypt and Lebanon.

The name Eudokia means 'good deeds,' for which she was widely known. Her name popped up in St. Nicholas Russian Orthodox Church as Euodacia. Surprisingly, this same sainted one's name is in the Greek Orthodox, Serbian Orthodox, Catholic church, and last but not least, she is also characterized as a Samaritan woman!

In researching her reputed residence in orthodoxy of Heliopolis, it was revealed that it is in Eastern Macedonia near Kabbalah, Greece. Macedonia is the area where all of the aforementioned women working with Paul were centered, as will be come more evident in the notes and historic quotations contained herein.

This Eudokia aka Euodacia led an initially sordid life. She was a filthy rich incorrigible harlot to put it bluntly. History has it that one night she overheard one Germanus, also known as Herman, witnessing to someone about the Final Judgment from the Bible. It frightened her so that she remained awake the balance of the night, no doubt pondering her errant lifestyle.

The next morning she sought Germanus (recall Hermes, Herman, Hermogenes, Hymaneus), heard his witness, and repented. She was converted immediately and disposed of all of her wealth to the poor as Jesus suggested to the rich, young ruler. Thereafter she was baptized and remained in residence earnestly studying and witnessing with two men for several months. After leaving, she practiced total abstinenece for the balance of her life, 56 years, and became an abbess or head over a group of celibate women or nuns.

Further study disclosed that she was a highly venerated woman, elevated by the Orthodox churches. She was known for remarkable grace, favor, and generosity, laying hands upon and healing the sick, converting individual sinners and entire regions while training others. She was most notably known for the gift of miracles, frequently calling upon the Lord and receiving an immediate positive response. She also trained others who raised the dead before she was beheaded.
https://www.gometropolis.org/orthodox-faith/feast-days/the-righteous-martyr-eudocia-the samaritan/;
https://www.orthodox.net/menaion-march/01-the-venerable-martyr-eudocia.html; https://oca.org/saints/lives/2010/03/01/100625-martyr-eudokia-of-heliopolis;
https://en.wikipedia.org/wiki/Eudokia_of_Heliopolis.

This woman was an Apostle in every sense of the word. The glory, grace, and power of God manifested in her as in our Euodia.

Whether the two women Euodia and Eudokia/Euodacia are one and the same or not, it is clear that someone with that name as a variant figured high on the ladder in the early church, bearing the characteristics if not the appellation of an apostle.

All of this lack of conclusive information, identity, and certainty are most unfortunate for every student of the Gospel. Everything that exists and is known at the present has been disclosed to you to make the decision for yourself as the jury viewing the facts.

Nonetheless, these women, Euodia and Syntyche, have their post in history amongst the apostolic church as workers with Paul, if not, in some minds, as actual Apostles.

CHAPTER 3

CHRISTIAN FAMILY FEUD: EUODIA AND SYNTYCHE (WHAT'S IT REALLY ALL ABOUT?)

Paul is between a rock and a hard place. A thriving ministry has a small scale, but rapidly escalating war in its midst. As fierce and committed as Euodia and Syntyche were to the Gospel, so they appeared to be in this rivalry. Whether the rivalry is with one another, as presumed by this author, or in dispute with the church or majority over a doctrinal issue, is unclear.

Paul tells them they are all his beloved, his joy and his crown, but this schism has to be reconciled. Philippians 2:2 KJV: Fulfil ye my joy that ye be likeminded, having the same love, being of one accord, of one mind.

PHILIPPIANS 4:1-2

Therefore, my brethren dearly beloved and longed for, my joy and crown, so stand fast in the Lord, my dearly beloved.

I beseech Euodia and Syntyche, that they be of the same mind in the Lord.

Arguments arise in churches today on another level. Whether behaving unseemly and yelling across the church as in Corinth, or disputing about covering of the head, what size hat is appropriate, the current distress over calling women in any capacity other than as missionaries or evangelists, whether pants, makeup, red lipstick, jewelry, speaking from the pulpit or the floor, the height of heels, respectability of peep toes, length of dress, to cover or not to cover the lap, sitting in the pulpit with the men, in the choir stand, off to the side with the Mother's Board or on the front row with the First Lady, the sheer presence of women in the ministry is decidedly the problem, *ESPECIALLY OUT OF THE MOUTHS OF WOMEN THEMSELVES*.

Let's take a brief look at what others have to say about strife, disagreements, and disputations.

It is noteworthy that in historical and philosophical writings, strife was considered an effeminate characteristic:

"There was not after all a single kind of strife, but on the earth two kinds, one of them a man might praise when he recognizes **her, but the other is blameworthy.***" Hesiod, Works and Days, c.700 B.C. 83:19.*

Why can't we, Euodia and Syntyche, emulate the Godhead? Strife is certainly not a Divine characteristic. We never hear of Father, Son, and

Holy Ghost having a tiff. They always agreed. In fact, they always say great and wonderful things about each other, like Father honoring Jesus at His Baptism and the Mount of Transfiguration: 'This is My Beloved Son in whom I AM well-pleased, (Hear ye Him)' or Jesus honoring Abba Father by obedience and submission: 'My meat is to accomplish the will of Him that sent Me' or Father sending the Holy Ghost at Jesus' request: 'I will pray to the Father and He will send you another COMFORTER…'. Matthew 3:17; Matthew 17; John 4:34; John 14:16 KJV.

More importantly, each member of the Godhead saw the other as necessary, vital, essential to the work and only suffered a schism when 'He Who knew no sin' became such for the saving of our souls. Even then, They were in agreement, just separated, *qodesh*, by His acquired sins.

God wants us, Euodia and Syntyche to be inseparable like They are (John 17 KJV). So great was the light of Their love that when They split, eternity will forever remark of the darkness that covered the face of the Earth. Eternity will always remember the earthquake that rent the heretofore invincible curtains that covered the ark and caused the dead to rise. GLORY. The womb of salvation was open and ready to deliver.

A less savory example of the lack of strife is satan. Except in cartoons, satan is not characterized as having trouble with his demons and minions (satan is never given the honor of capitalization in any of this author's works).

Strife is cast as an effeminate and a decidedly 'human' thing.

'For ye are yet carnal, for whereas there is among you envying and strife, divisions, are ye not carnal and walk as **men**?' I Corinthians 3:3; James 4:1 KJV.

On the other hand, strife, under the right circumstances, over the right issues and appropriate audience, can be a healthy thing as when you debate an issue. *Heraclitus, Diogenes Laertius, Lives of Eminent Philosophers, bk. IX, sec.8, 46:15 and Plato, Cratylus, 402A c.540-c.480 B.C.*

The opposite is beneficial; from things that differ comes the fairest attunement; all things are born through strife.

Proverbs 25:8 KJV:

'Go not forth hastily to strive lest thou know not what to do in the end thereof when thy neighbor hath put thee to shame. Debate thy cause with thy neighbor himself and discover not a secret to another. Lest he that heareth it put thee to shame and thine infamy turn not away.'

Clearly, that is what has happened here. These two women of God had an issue with one another or with the rest of the church and it got out of hand. They were 'going at it.' News of it spread like wildfire. It reached Paul. It apparently was not 'if you find thy brother taken in a fault, go to him'...and if he will not hear you then take another and if that doesn't work, take it before the church. Matthew 18:15-17; Galatians 6:1 KJV. Nope.

James 4:1 KJV From whence come wars and fights among you, come they not hence, even from your lusts which war against your members?

A. Law vs. Grace / Faith

Paul's prior admonitions evolve around the issues of law versus righteousness by faith. This was preceded by the argument over circumcision and apparently 'who's running things' and deciding in Paul's absence. This is one of the prospects for the source of the argument between Euodia and Syntyche.

Paul uses the same language in Philippians as he does in dealing with prior legalistic issues.

Remember Paul's warning in Philippians 3:15 KJV:

Let us therefore as many as be thus minded (seeking the prize in Christ v. 14); and if in anything ye be otherwise minded, God shall reveal even this unto you.

The issue of circumcision is also at stake in this debate as demonstrated in the back reference to (Philippians 3:1-4 KJV) Galatians 5:4 KJV-

Christ becomes of no effect in you, whosoever of you are justified by the law, ye are fallen from grace.

For we through the Spirit wait for the hope of righteousness by faith.

For in Jesus Christ neither circumcision availeth anything nor uncircumcision; but faith which worketh by love (yet, Paul had Timothy circumsised!!!).

Ye did run well; who did hinder you that ye should not obey the truth?

This persuasion cometh not of Him that calleth you.

A little leaven leaveneth the whole lump.

I have confidence in you through the Lord that ye will be none otherwise minded...

Proverbs 20:3 KJV:

It is an honor for a man to cease from strife, but every fool will be meddling.

That Euodia and Syntyche were influential and extraordinary in the fellowship of those ministering there is evident since Paul personally crafted the letter with the aid of Timothy and sought one of the brethren to quash the dispute before it infected the entire tribe.

The 'true yokefellow' sent with the Pauline letter to the women was thought to be either Timothy, Silas, or Epaphroditus by scholars Peter Toon and William Barclay. However, Timothy assisted in the writing of the letter (Philippians 1:1 KJV) and Epaphroditus was the courier as well as the local Pastor. *The Oxford Orations of Dr. John Owen, Ed. Peter Toon, Callington (Cornwall): Gospel Communication (1971) ISBN 978-0-*

9501252-1-3 ; William Barclay, *"The Letters to the Philippians, Colossians, and Thessalonians"*, The St. Andrew Press (Edinburgh), Revised Edition 1975, page 74.

That Euodia and Syntyche rose to something short of a raucous that warranted the others' intervention makes one lean to the aforementioned hypothesis that the dispute was over something integral to the Gospel or worship. Circumcision was definitely one of the issues brewing at the time.

Remember Paul's warning in Philippians 3:15 KJV:

Let us therefore as many as be thus minded (seeking the prize in Christ v. 14); and if in anything ye be otherwise minded, God shall reveal even this unto you.

Paul persistently and unabashedly, repeatedly directs them to the Author and Finisher of our faith. Yet, Christ said I came not to destroy the Law and the Prophets, but to fulfill them.

Every aspect of Christ's ministry and being copy and supersede the utensils and furnishings of the Tabernacle and the Ark of the Covenant. Pursuing His Presence, Intimacy With God Revealed in the Tabernacle (Whittaker House _____) by David Cerullo; 7 Blessings of the Atonement (Refuge Productions) by Steve Munsey.

Notice that Paul's personal plight of incarceration did not stop him from focusing on the need for peace, the preeminence of the Gospel, the joy of the Lord, love and following in Christ's footsteps of humility. This great charge could not be reduced to a brawl over circumcision and the law. If the enemy could get Euodia and Syntyche and us stuck on such nonissues, we will not 'follow after' and come to a full knowledge of the Truth.

For our conversation is in heaven, from whence also we look for the Saviour, the Lord Jesus Christ. Philippians 3:20 KJV.

After all, Paul was keenly aware that he had once been Saul consenting to the death of others and deserving to die himself. His every breath was a testament to God's grace. He knew the enemy was trying to entice Euodia, Syntyche, and now us to commit spiritual homicide by legalistic distractions. Of a truth, that much has not changed!

Paul, having been spared a death he truly deserved, understood the treasure. The earthen vessel did not matter whether it be Balaam's ass (Numbers 21-22 KJV), the colt, the foal of an ass (Genesis 49:10, Matthew 21:2,5,7 KJV), a Liz Taylor at the well (John 4:6 KJV), a leper (Luke 17:12 KJV), a woman with a 12-year issue (Mark 5:25 KJV), a man waiting for an angel to move water once per year for 38 years in Solomon's portico (John 5:1), a blind man and his parents (John 9:6), Legion (Mark 5:9 KJV), a roof raising paralytic and his carriers (Mark 2 KJV), covert Nicodemus (John 3:1 KJV), or height challenged Zaccheus (Luke 19), Mary Magdalen (Matthew 27:56 KJV), the women first at the tomb (Mark 16 KJV), lying, cursing Peter (Matthew 26:69 KJV), Paul (Acts 9), or Apollos (I Cor. 1:12)… THE MESSAGE IS WHAT MATTERS! THE VESSEL IS INCONSEQUENTIAL. God provides the increase.

This battle in Philippi over law, grace, faith, circumcision, uncircumcision, authority, leadership, is nothing short of a satanic ruse of distraction.

B. The Motivation for Serving/Ministering

A second plausible basis of the discord between Euodia and Syntyche is Paul's stern but evidently necessary admonition about motives in preaching the Gospel. It had to be Jesus or nothing. Pride and self-promotion have no place in this good news program. That's a four-week preaching series by itself:

Philippians 1:15-18 KJV:

Some indeed preach Christ even from envy and strife, and some also from good will: the former preach Christ from selfish ambition, not sincerely supposing to add affliction to my chains; but the latter out of love, knowing that I am appointed for the defense of the Gospel. What then? Only that in every way, whether in pretense or in truth, Christ is preached; and in this, I rejoice, yes, and will rejoice.

Paul is hitting an area that causes hours of debate even now. It is not about our egos, our reputation, the size of the offering, the numbers in attendance, or who can gain the preeminence. To Paul, the end does not justify the means. It's about fruit. It's about righteousness. It's about being pleasing in the sight of the Good Shepherd, the Ancient of Days, the Author, and Finisher of our faith. While Paul was incarcerated, they demonstrated immaturity, jealousy, envy, strife, competitiveness all of which would conceivably bring shame to the cause of Christ.

Having thus stated, Paul reaches the same conclusion as Christ when the early disciples challenged the right of the others who preached, but not as part of their group. Paul determined as Christ, *let it ride!* Whatever their motives in preaching, Christ was gaining notoriety. Men meant it for evil, God meant it for good. Unruliness and disputations were adding pressure and unjust credence to the accusations against him and to Paul's reputation with the authorities. He would make himself of no reputation like Christ, His Savior, Mentor, and Role-Model. Philippians 2:3 KJV.

Philippians 2:14-18 KJV:

Do all things without complaining and disputing, that you may become blameless and harmless children of God without fault in the midst of a crooked and perverse generation, among whom you shine as lights in the world, holding fast the WORD OF LIFE, so that I may rejoice in the day of Christ that I have not run in vain or labored in vain. Yes, and I am being poured out as a drink offering on the sacrifice and service of your faith, I am glad and rejoice with you all. For the same reason, you also be glad and rejoice with me.

For those who may have doubted the positions Euodia and

Syntyche held in the body, Paul certainly would not be going to these lengths to remind them who they are. He is gently shifting them back into propriety and faith as he did Timothy when he told him to stir up the gifts that lie within him by the laying on of hands and reminds him of the faith of his mother and grandmother, Eunice and Lois. 2 Timothy 1:5 KJV.

Paul has the same apostolic purpose, just a different tactic. He knows his people. Paul is aware strategically of what to say to get Euodia and Syntyche back on track so the Gospel train can continue on its unimpeded journey.

We, too, must know those with whom we labor. Christ didn't just break bread with the disciples as often as He did because they were hungry. He wanted to know who they were and to help them learn one another. Three years, Christ nurtured them and let them see every aspect of His life, His mother, brethren, sisters, prayer life, ministerial approaches, eating habits, fasting, sleeping, detractors, sweat, tears. Nothing was hidden from them. Paul practices the same transparency with Euodia, Syntyche, and the others. He follows Christ's pristine example. If there is an issue, if there is a bone of contention, a dispute, the resolution of it lies in the Word of God says Paul. He says 'I am a true representative because I follow in the footsteps of Christ and urge you, Euodia and Syntyche, to do likewise'.

I Corinthians 1:6 KJV-

Howbeit we speak wisdom among them that are perfect; yet not the wisdom of this world, nor of the princes of this world, that come to naught:

But we speak the wisdom of God in a mystery, even the hidden wisdom, which God ordained before the world unto our glory.

Which none of the princes of this world knew for had they known, they would not have crucified the Lord of Glory.

But as it is written, Eye hath not seen, nor ear heard, neither hath entered into the heart of man, the things which God hath prepared for them that love Him.

But God hath revealed them unto us by His Spirit; for the Spirit searcheth all things, yea the deep things of God.

What God has prepared is inextricably, invariably intertwined with His Only Begotten Son, the Firstborn from the dead who 'they that worship, must worship Him in Spirit and in truth.'

In fact, *HE IS WHAT GOD HAS PREPARED* as HE DEPOSITED HIM IN MARY'S WOMB VIA THE HOVERING OR OVERSHADOWING OF THE HOLY SPIRIT (**AND, NO! CARNAL ONES, NOT BY INTERCOURSE).** Jesus departed so that the Spirit of Truth, the Holy Ghost would come, place us under His Tutelage as the Second Paraclete, and open our eyes to the Truth of Christ----Christ, the fullness of the Godhead bodily!

Let us follow after and choose to be led.

In the world, YE SHALL HAVE TRIBULATION. BE OF GOOD CHEER, I HAVE OVERCOME THE WORLD.

CHAPTER 4

SATAN, THE GENESIS OF STRIFE

As stated in the Introduction, we will venture off into the origins of strife and how Paul deals with it. Let's go.

Webster's defines war:

werra, strife, akin to *werran* to confuse, *werrere*, to sweep; a state of unusual open, declared, hostile conflict between states or nations....

2a. a state of hostility, conflict or antagonism;

    b. a struggle between opposing forces for a particular end. Webster's New Collegiate Dictionary, G & C Merriam Company (1973).

Even the best of us can get side-tracked, distracted, off of the beaten path, out of alignment. Each time satan sets you up to stray, just remember he is after your identity. He is a sponge. When God says who you are and thereby crowns you with identity and purpose, satan steps in with a vicious, though seemingly innocuous, set of questions: "If thou be…" and "Hast God said?" He wants to set your mind into chaos and ultimately destroy your relationship and communion with the Godhead. He tried it on Jesus. Luke 4 KJV so you are not exempt. He takes the same measures in separating Euodia and Syntyche so it behooves us to examine the strategy.

Proverbs 3:30 KJV states, 'strive not with a man without cause.' Proverbs 17:14 KJV adds, 'the beginning of strife is as when one letteth out water; therefore leave off contention before it be meddled with.'

It does not take long for a fire to spread and disrupt the Divine Order as we see from this paraphrased excerpt from Genesis, 'The Beginning:'

"OF COURSE IT'S HER FAULT, AND YOU MADE HER!"

This Adamic complaint was first, not the murmuring of the Israelites in the wilderness.

By the choice of God, Woman was tenderly and carefully formed from the side of man AND was given DOMINION WITH HIM. Genesis 2:18 KJV. Man did not *ask* for her. God determined that having her served man's best interests.

Man was formed with love by LOVE (Genesis 1:26-27; 2:7 KJV). This same Love Personified deemed it inappropriate for a man to be alone. Love pulled Woman and crafted her from a rib of man's side and breathed the Ruach Hakodesh into them. That breath was also love. They became living (and conceivably loving) souls and were given dominion over everything God made (Genesis 2:19, 21-25 KJV). Their Creator is the First Apostle. The Godhead formed her and Adam from the pre-created dust of the Earth. Adam first, then Woman from

Adam, making them uniquely designed life, infused with Their life---Their breath.

Until recently, women have been relegated to the back of the bus, the back seat, a second class citizen, a nonentity in education, church, the professions, arts, economics, media, entertainment, business, and government---all of the mountains, except family (Genesis 1:26-27; 2:7;2:21-22 KJV. *Junia Arise*, Apostle Axel Sippach Alpha Publishing, 2018).

Moreover, they had daily face to face, one on one communication and communion with God, fellowship and intimacy with clearly-defined instructions or parameters.

It is true, woman blew it with satan in the garden. Distracted by the sweet talk, like Delilah in reverse, she let her guard down. She allowed satan to engage her in a contest (vain disputation) of words. This was really a deceptive design to challenge the WORD OF GOD, which is the Son of God. He wanted to seize the authority and dominion he lost when he was evicted from on High:

How art thou fallen from heaven, O Lucifer, son of the morning.

How art thou cut down to the ground which didst weaken the nations!

For thou hast said in thine heart, I will ascend into heaven. I will exalt my throne above the stars of God; I will sit also upon the Mount of the Congregation, in the sides of the north.

I will ascend above the height of the clouds; I will be like the Most High.

Yet thou shalt be brought down to hell to the sides of the pit (Isaiah 14:12-15 KJV).

Strife comes when one attempts to assert or force one's will upon or over another's. Sometimes, as with satan's insurrection here, that other is God or the known will of God as set forth in His Holy Word.

Euodia and Syntyche as set forth above were contending for preeminence over either a matter of law versus grace or motivation in ministering the Word. It's the same cake with different icing as the Edenic debacle.

Woman fell for it. satan had the advantage of thousands of years of experience, but she clearly understood the import of 'Hast God said…' Genesis 3:1 KJV. This is the first recorded "double dog dare ya!"

Adam and Woman had the secrets of the Lord revealed to them because they feared Him, then they lost it. She convinced her husband to partake of the forbidden fruit and lost that Godlink in one fell swoop. They were apprentice architects, working hand in hand with the Chief Architect and reaped an eviction notice for their egregious disobedience.

We speak today of how the love of many has waxed cold, but is that new? Adam and Woman were part of God's intimate Starbucks daily fellowship. Yet, they turned against Him. Friendship with the world is enmity with God (James 4:4 KJV).

The carnal mind is enmity (Romans 8:7 KJV). It was the carnal mind, the lust of the eyes, the flesh and pride (Nobody tells me I can't) that led Woman to debate and then disdain God's rule and eat of the fruit:

"Let us walk honestly as in the day…not in strife and envying. But put on the Lord Jesus Christ and make no provision for the flesh to fulfill the lusts thereof" (Romans 13:13 KJV).

The heart-wrenching part was not just in the lack of loving Him, but faulting Him for compassion and foresight in creating her. This is what Isaiah refers to as the putting forth of the finger of accusation (Isaiah 58:9 KJV)---when the man (Adam) said (Genesis 3:12 KJV) 'The woman **WHOM THOU GAVEST TO BE WITH ME'**, she gave me of the tree and *I did eat*. That must have stabbed God right in the heart! Assuming for a moment a human mentality, it would have left Him reeling like a drunk hit by the ballast of a ship.

Strife and accusation number 2: …And the woman said, the serpent beguiled me, and *I did eat.* Excuse me, how is this serpent, Johnny-come-lately going to pop up out of nowhere and talk smack to you about your directives from the God who made, daily communes with you, and gave you everything? Yet, satan does it all of the time. He gets in that ear gate and has a field day (See James W. Goll on The Deaf and Dumb Spirit).

The bottom line is not what either God or the serpent did. The real deal problem is what Adam and Eve said: ***"AND I DID EAT."*** The disobedience was volitional. A conscious decision was made to hurt the ONE WHO loved them. Had it been put in those terms, they probably would not have done it. Neither would we, but the net effect is the same.

God did not get mad, He quickly cleaned house. Since the serpent wanted what Adam and Woman had, he was consigned to his belly so he can enjoy the diet of dust. He is 'blessed to eat' the same dust from which those he sought to devour were created. God has a way of making His point stick.

The end result was lies, deceit (Genesis 3:6-9 KJV), severance of the union, trust and sweet communion between God and mankind, and the disruption of the family as we know it (Genesis 3:16-17 KJV).

Euodia and Syntyche's debate caused disruption in the Christian family as well.

Man would be engulfed in deriving a living by the sweat of his brow from unyielding earth. Woman was cursed to incessant travail in childbirth, the threat of the serpent at the heel of her seed, and subjection to her husband.

EVERYTHING that Christ did upon the Earth--- from the capacity to commune with our Heavenly Father on mountaintops, feeding the sheep, tending the lamb, casting out devils, healing the sick, raising the dead, exercising authority over all of the power of the enemy---all of this was given to man to do 'greater works than these' in all nations (Mark 16, Luke 9:1-2; Luke 10:19; Acts 1:8 KJV).

God did not preclude Woman from the same undertakings. Christ is no respecter of persons. There is neither male nor female, Jew nor Gentile, bond nor free (Galatians 3:28 KJV). All are Christ's and Christ is God's (Ephesians 1:22-23 KJV).

CHAPTER 5

ME TOO?! LAYING THE BLAME AT GOD'S FEET

Strife inevitably evolves from the blame game as well. No one wants to be responsible for what goes amiss so we shove the responsibility into another's face. Who's doing who in the case of Euodia and Syntyche, or is it mutual faultfinding?

Since we are addressing issues evolving around the Apostolic or another call of women, the displaced blame for the calling, the stigma attached to it, and having realized that the first such accusation was leveled by Adam; it is only fitting to address the Sovereignty of God versus the finite human understanding (Isaiah 55 KJV).

When we fight over the call of women, we display the same level of foolishness and distraction as the legalistic issue of circumcision. Thus the Gospel is set aside while we war over the flesh and souls die.

THE WORD IS CLEAR, EVEN THE VERY FOOLISHNESS OF GOD IS WISER THAN MEN. YET WE PRESUME TO TELL HIM WHO HE CAN AND CANNOT CALL. REALLY?

I Corinthians 1:26 KJV:

For ye see your calling brethren, how that not many wise men after the flesh, not many mighty, not many noble are called;

But God hath chosen the foolish things of the world to confound the wise; and God hath chosen the weak things of the world to confound the things which are mighty.

And the base things of the world, and things which are despised hath God chosen, yea and things which are not, to bring to naught things that are.

THAT NO FLESH SHOULD GLORY IN HIS PRESENCE! (emphasis supplied)

Let's deal with the foolishness or presumptuous reproach of God for worthless selections first (I Corinthians 1:26 KJV). This discussion is purely from the standpoint of man's perspective on God's handling of God's own affairs since we know that God is not only Perfect, Omniscient, Omnipresent, Holy and cannot fail or lie.

Spiro Zodiates Key Hebrew Greek Study Bible defines foolishness as *'morologia'* from the word *'monos',* meaning foolishness, or perhaps recklessness or mindlessness of work or of speech. Foolish talking in such a manner that it demonstrates or reflects the nature of a person.

The second term is *'moros'* as in silly, stupid, foolish (moron), reckless, referring to scorn of the mental processes as in *'raca'*, stupidity; scorn of the heart and character; foolish, ignorant, salt that has lost its savor, personal quality, and not just periodic idle talk.

Misled souls might sit in the seat of the scornful of God deeming Him 'foolish':

- in being merciful and marking an unrepentant Cain- (Genesis 4 KJV);
- sending Jonah to the Ninevites knowing Nahum saw their impending destruction- (Jonah 3:10-4:3 KJV);
- the quintessential Jeremiah having to flee in a basket let down on the side of a wall- (Jeremiah 38:11-13 KJV);
- the choice of Rahab the harlot to cover the spies and promise to spare her entire household to satisfy the debt… (Joshua 2:1-25 KJV) we won't even discuss her in Jesus' bloodline;
- utilizing Esther the orphaned to be a concubine to a drunken king to rescue her people (Esther 2:15-20; Esther 5 KJV);
- the numerous times Moses and Aaron were sent to Pharoah while God hardened his heart (Exodus 5-11 KJV), which is right up there with the trips of the poor servant of Elijah looking for a cloud (I Kings 18:41-45 KJV);
- parting the Red Sea, healing Mara, feeding them manna, quail, coriander while letting them wander in the wilderness 40 years (Exodus 14:21; Exodus16 KJV);
- parting the Jordan (Joshua 3:1- KJV);
- not allowing David to clean Saul's clock because Saul was 'still the Lord's anointed' (I Samuel 26 KJV);
- Jonathan and his servant crawling between Bozez and Seneth fighting the Philistines while Saul pontificated under a pomegranate tree---mind you this is the second failure because David had to handle the Philistines first with a slingshot and

five smooth stones while Saul watched (I Samuel 14; I Samuel 17 KJV);
- taking a child's lunch of two fish and five loaves to feed 5,000 plus women and children (Matthew 14:17 KJV);
- using Elijah to use meal to remove poison from a prophetic vegetable medley feast (2 Kings 4:38-41 KJV);
- Ezekiel speaking to dry bones (Ezekiel 37 KJV);
- sparing not His only begotten Son, allowing His crucifixion to save wretches like us (Matthew 27:50 KJV).

Part II, the weakness of God is stronger than men:

The word for weakness is *asthenia, astheneo, asthenia, astheneses* without *stenos* or strength; weakness, sickness in the whole of a person or a part thereof; impotence, economic weakness or literal poverty; to be infirm, sick, weak, spiritually devoid or diminished as in the faith, destitute of authority, dignity, power, indignant, contemptible.

If there be any alleged weakness in God it is in loving us, sparing not His own Son and delivering Him up for us all.

Some presumed demonstrations of God's weakness:
- in not destroying us for building the tower of Babel (Genesis 11 KJV), Noah's flood (Genesis 8 KJV), Korah's rebellion (Numbers 16 KJV), the strange fire on the altar;
- refusal to go up to the feast on Palm Sunday with His brothers (John 7 KJV);
- foot-washing (John 13 KJV);
- the Last Supper (Matthew 26:17 KJV);
- Jesus suffering Judas betrayal (Matthew 26:14-16, 23 KJV);
- Jesus' sweat like blood in the Garden of Gethsemane (Matthew 26:36; Mark 14:32; Luke 22:40KJV);

- Jesus' arrest and trial before Herod and Pilate (Matthew 26:47-27:14 KJV);
- Jesus took 39 stripes Matthew 27:26-28 KJV);
- Jesus (Matthew 27:27-29 KJV) crowned with thorns, crimson robe, "Hail King of the Jews";
- enduring the mockery of the thief 'If Thou be the Son of God...?' (Matthew 27:40 KJV);
- compelled to carry the cross until Simon came (Matthew 27:32 KJV);
- spittle and plucked His beard;
- Father forgive them for they ***KNOW NOT WHAT THEY DO! (Luke 23:34 KJV)***.

LET THIS MIND BE IN YOU WHICH WAS ALSO IN CHRIST JESUS;

WHO BEING IN THE FORM OF GOD THOUGHT IT NOT ROBBERY TO BE EQUAL WITH GOD

BUT MADE HIMSELF OF NO REPUTATION, AND TOOK UPON HIM THE FORM OF A SERVANT, AND WAS MADE IN THE LIKENESS OF MEN;

AND BEING FOUND IN FASHION AS A MAN, HE HUMBLED HIMSELF AND BECAME OBEDIENT UNTO DEATH, EVEN THE DEATH OF THE CROSS. Philippians 2:5-8 KJV (emphasis supplied)

Isaiah 53:10 Yet it pleased the Lord to bruise Him; He hath put Him to grief...

The weakness is strength and the foolishness is wise when you consider: Philippians 2:9 KJV.

WHEREFORE GOD HATH HIGHLY EXALTED HIM AND GIVEN HIM A NAME THAT IS ABOVE EVERY NAME. (emphasis supplied)

This section hopefully fulfilled a twofold purpose. For those called women who question God's use of them and other women and speak of the futility and impossibility of it all, look again. Look at the life of Christ and what He endured. Better yet, look at His death and the eternal blessing of His Resurrection and know that in ministering under fire, you have joined His August Presence and the team of the elite.

For the men who have made it their business to harass, attack, ridicule, undermine, and destroy the works of called women, know that you run the risk of being found to be fighting against God. That is definitely not a wholesome place to be. ***HE IS SOVEREIGN!***

CHAPTER 6

STRIFE DEVOURS TRIBES. HERE'S THE SOLUTION.

The Oxford study Bible cross-references strife when researching the word quarreling or quarrelsome!

Referring once again to Webster's:

1 a. a bitter sometimes violent conflict or dissension;

   b. an act of contention: fight or struggle;

2. exertion or contention for superiority

3. archaic: earnest endeavor or discord

Let nothing be done through strife or vainglory, but in lowliness of mind. let each esteem the other better than themselves. Look not every man on his own things, but every man also on the things of others (Philippians 2:2 KJV).

Follow peace with all men and holiness, without which no man can see the Lord. Looking diligently lest any man fails of the grace of God; lest any root of bitterness springing up trouble you and thereby many be defiled (Romans 12:14-15 KJV).

This is what love is. Be not high minded but condescend to men of low estate (Romans12:16 KJV):

Be of the same mind one toward another. Mind not high things, but condescend to men of low estate. Be not wise in your own conceits.

God's command to us when strife arises is quite simple: FAST!

Isaiah 58:4-12 KJV:

Behold ye fast for strife and debate, and to smite with the fist of wickedness; ye shall not fast as ye do this day, to make your voice be heard on high.

Is it such a fast that I have chosen? A day for a man to afflict his soul? Is it to bow down his head as a bulrush, and to spread sackcloth and ashes under him? Wilt thou call this a fast, an acceptable day unto the Lord?

Is not this the fast that I have chosen? To <u>lose</u> the bands of wickedness, to <u>undo</u> the heavy burdens, and <u>to let</u> the oppressed go free, and that ye <u>break</u> every yoke?

Is it not to <u>deal</u> thy bread to the hungry, and that thou <u>bring</u> the poor that are cast out to thy house? when thou seest the naked, that thou <u>cover</u> him; and that thou <u>hide not</u> thyself from thine own flesh?

Then shall thy light break forth as the morning, and thine health shall spring forth speedily and thy righteousness shall go before thee; the glory of the Lord shall be thy rearward.

Then shalt thou call and the Lord shall answer; thou shalt cry and He shall say 'here I am". If thou take away from the midst of thee the yoke, the putting forth of the finger, and speaking vanity;

And if thou draw out thy soul to the hungry; and satisfy the afflicted soul; then shall thy light rise in obscurity, and thy darkness be as the noonday:

And the Lord shall guide thee continually, and satisfy thy soul in drought, and make fat thy bones and thou shalt be like a watered garden, and like a spring of water, whose waters fail not.

And they that shall be of thee shall build the old waste places; thou shalt raise up the foundations of many generations; and thou shalt be called, the Repairer of the Breach. The Restorer of the Paths to dwell in.

God tells us through the sagacious Isaiah in Isaiah 58 and in Psalms 58 KJV, as well, that the solution to strife is fasting. Fasting puts the flesh in subjection. Surprisingly, Paul did not mention this in his letter to Euodia and Syntyche!

Most, but not all of the time, strife is prideful and due to someone pushing for preeminence or recognition.

God says the prescription is simple. Lose the bands of wickedness or stop forcing your way and will. Next, to undo heavy burdens means to stop being Pharisaical, having people shoulder rules and loads that you would not follow or lift. Breaking yokes testifies that the only yoke-placer is God Himself. Everyone else lacks authority. His yoke is easy and His burden is light.

The next four prescriptions are proactive. Deal your bread or feed the poor. Bring the poor into your house, don't leave them outside like my Son at His birth. Provide cover meaning supply whatever they need. Hide not from your own flesh because but for My Grace, this could very well be you!

There are eight solutions. Eight is the number of new beginnings. God says that if you do these eight things, you shall have three things. They are the receipt, the blessing, symbolizing the Trinity.

The first is to have light, that is God Himself based upon Revelations. There shall be no need for the sun nor moon to give light. You shall have righteousness, which was purchased by the blood of the lamb. Glory shall be your portion and we know that glory represents the presence of the Holy Ghost, the Shekinah Glory.

Once these things are in place, saving souls, leading many to righteousness, restoring the streets, the paths to dwell in, will be less difficult. Why? God will no longer turn a deaf ear. He will answer when you call. Hallelujah!

Daniel 12:3 KJV:

And they that be wise shall shine as the brightness of the firmament, and they that turn many to righteousness, as the stars forever and ever.

Paul (Philippians 4 KJV) has a fivefold solution to this first level (apostolic) fivefold (2 is agreement; 5 is mercy or favor Number in Scripture, E.W. Bullinger, Kregel Publications 1867, 1964) problem:

Stand firm and Rejoice always as set forth in Philippians 4 KJV. *Stand firm* meaning to not waffle or waver with every wind and wave of doctrine (James 1 KJV). Stand fast in the liberty as well as the doctrine wherewith Christ has made us free. Where the Spirit of the Lord is there is liberty (2 Corinthians 3:17 KJV). He whom the Son sets free shall be free indeed (John 8:32 KJV). Don't revert to the bondage of legalism. Temptations may abound with all kinds of Greek gods, fetishes, and festivals. Therefore, Paul tells Euodia, Syntyche and the others, stay focused. Don't give any place to satan.

The stand firm reminds us of the full armor of God (Ephesians 6 KJV). Don it, the helmet of salvation, breastplate of righteousness, loins girt with truth, feet shod with the preparation of the Gospel of peace, the sword of the Spirit and the shield of faith, or use your slingshot and five smooth stones (I Samuel 17:50 KJV). Whatever it takes, don't let the division fester. Don't let the sun go down on your wrath as it apparently had already with Euodias and Syntyche.

Rejoice always. My grace is sufficient for you. My strength is made perfect in your weakness (2 Corinthians 12:9 KJV). In other words, don't focus on the problem, focus on the Problem-Solver who says, 'My peace I give unto you, not as the world gives, give I unto you.' *The Interpreter's Bible Commentary, Volume 11, Abingdon Press.*

Also be **bearers of light**, worthy representatives of the 'Light of the World' (see Matthew 5:14 KJV). Maintaining a healthy concept of self-identity and 'job description', purpose, or assignment is essential to the Body of Christ.

John 1:12-13 KJV:

But as many as received Him, to them gave He the power to become the sons of God, even to them that believe on His name; which were born not of blood, nor of the will of the flesh, nor of the will of man, but of God.

They are to be **faultless and blameless** as set forth above, without spot or wrinkle, hating even the garments stained by the flesh.

They are to be vessels of honor, vessels of holiness unto the Lord.

Finally, they are *to hold fast* to the WORD OF LIFE, the Gospel, their profession of faith.

Quite a tall order to fulfill? Not at all! Au contraire. They were given ***THE POWER, EXOUSIA.*** They had authority delegated by God. They had influence, charisma, **DOMINION**, kratos, dunamis. These are the seal, the proof, of our inheritance as credible as tokens of virginity to a bridegroom.

'Go ye, therefore.'

CHAPTER 7

MOVING TOWARD A UNIFIED HOUSE

CAST NOT AWAY THY CONFIDENCE WHICH HATH GREAT RECOMPENSE OF REWARD. This does not mean hold your ground and divide the house! Hebrews 10:35; Ruth 2:12; 2 Samuel 22:21; Ps. 18:12 Matthew 12:25; Mark 3:24; Luke 11:17 KJV. "House" or household" (of faith) includes the Kingdom family. We are built, stone upon stone, as a house for the Living Trinity.

Brethren is **Achim,** which can refer to countrymen, neighbors, friends, or relatives. Quite frankly, it extends to any other human! We are our brother's keeper as Elohim told Cain and as Jesus explained to His disciples although He further refined it to 'those who do the will of My Father.' Matthew 12:48-50 KJV

We are to stick together, remain together or abide with one another as we abide in him (John 15 KJV). The church in Acts grasped this and was, therefore, productive and spiritually blessed on the day of Pentecost and thereafter. It is the mirror image of John 15.

God has committed the ministry of reconciliation unto us. We cannot say that we love Him and not be at peace with our brothers and sisters (see Matthew 5:24 KJV). The entirety of the Gospel is that God was in Christ (John 17 KJV) reconciling the world unto Himself (Romans 5:10; Ephesians 2:16 KJV).

Reconciliation is the gist of all of Acts, Pentecost, what we see in the Holy Trinity, and the Holy aspiration for the Bride.

This same reconciliation is Paul's goal with Euodia and Syntyche. They are Paul's joy because he has fed and watched them grow from babes in Christ to 'fellow laborers' and 'yokefellows', inferring side by side laborers, perhaps equals. They have labored, sweat, eaten, slept, and been persecuted for the cause of Christ. What could draw them any closer? Perhaps it was Paul's absence due to imprisonment that left the door cracked for the division. Perhaps without the head, they suffered: Smite the shepherd and the sheep shall be scattered (Matthew 26:31 KJV).

Notice, despite all that is transpiring, Paul operates above the fray. **FIRST a word of encouragement and hope---they are not only his beloved and joy but also his crown.** The joy is now. The crown also refers to now, but more to later indicating Paul's full expectation that what he is beseeching in the name of Christ shall be complied with. It also speaks of Paul's conclusion about their future---'their names are written in the Book of Life.' Contrary to popular belief, it is not in poor taste to speak your informed view of the future destination of those about you.

Additionally, there is Paul's undaunted faith that He that hath begun a good work in them will see it through to completion (Philippians 1:6 KJV). They too run the race, not battling the air, but to obtain a crown. As Paul spoke to the Galatians, Are ye so foolish Having begun in the Spirit, are ye now made perfect by the flesh (Galatians 3:3)?

Herein lies a lesson for most, especially Pastors. Though it grips and even rends your heart, don't jump out and react while you are still in heat, hurt, and unresolved over the issue of misconduct or rebellion. Don't wait too long, but make sure you let the dust settle and seek the Lord while He may be found and call upon Him while He is near.

We are but UNDER-shepherds, while He is the King of Kings and Lord of Lords. The sheep are His, as is the crown. Remember the wisdom of Solomon in the battle between two mothers over the remaining live baby?

What crown are the congregations we serve and the staff we train, license, and ordain to us? Perhaps a garland, a wreath of victory for assisting in calling them out of the darkness and into His marvelous light. A battle, yes, but not a game. This war waged and raging with satan is far from a game or contest at a Greek festival.

Frequently those we minister to or share the fivefold with, also pierce, sting, and draw blood like a crown of thorns. Look at the role of Judas, steadily alongside Jesus, privy to all of His business, but a betrayer. Look at Peter, cursing and denying Him as the others did in fleeing upon His arrest. Consider John who laid upon His chest but followed 'afar off' to see what would become of Him. Ah! James and John, Zebedee's sons, desirous of seats of prominence and preeminence upon the right and left of Christ, imploring their mother to force His hand.

Apostles must douse the false fire with the water of the Word. Though Paul was gentle with these women, it is bred of his apparent respect for them and the extent and quality of their prior labors.

He is far from diplomatic with Hermogenes (2 Timothy 1:5 KJV), Hymaenus (1 Timothy 1; 2 Timothy 2 KJV), Philetus (2 Timothy 2:17-18 KJV), and Alexander (I Timothy 1:19-20 KJV). He treats them like the demonized and blasphemous reprobates that they have become.

Paul cautions Timothy to wage a good warfare, hold the faith and a good conscience. Philippians 2:20-21 KJV. These others Paul says have become a shipwreck concerning the faith. Paul says that they have been 'delivered unto satan, that they may learn not to blaspheme.' I Timothy 1:18-20 KJV.

Paul attacks Hymaneus, Hermogenes, Philetus, and Alexander for 'false doctrine'---'vain and profane babblings' that 'will lead to further ungodliness'. 'And their word will eat as does a canker of whom is Hymenaeus and Philetus, who concerning the truth have erred saying that the Resurrection is past already and overthrow the faith of some' (II Timothy 2:16-18 KJV).

The implications of such erroneous teaching are far-reaching. If the resurrection is past, their holiness, hope, and faith are wasted. They may as well eat, drink, and be merry because their hoped for Savior and eternal life are but a vapor in a memory. This teaching is akin to those today who say that there are no more gifts and administrations of the Holy Spirit because 'that which is perfect has already come' (see I Corinthians 13 KJV). The Holy Spirit is our tutor, to lead and guide us into all truth and put us in remembrance until Christ returns the second time. Yet, some persist in error and blaspheme against the Holy Ghost like those that said Jesus cast out demons by Beelzebub!

It is rather ironic that Philetus' name connotes 'beloved'; but he is listed amongst the betrayers of Paul, blasphemers of the Holy Ghost, leading others astray and thereby causing divisiveness in the tribe.

There is a very clear, unequivocal demarcation here. Euodia and Syntyche, as more fully discussed herein, were in earnest, though turbulent debate. Paul dealt with them differently from those who wrangled the Word and caused others to fall. He consigned the wranglers to satan! The Truth has no favorites. Neither should we as leaders, Apostles, Pastors. If there is a foul ball, call it out.

Something else is at stake here:

Hebrews 13:7 KJV:

Remember them which have the rule over you, who have spoken unto you the Word of God whose faith follow considering the end of their conversation.

Hebrews 13:17 KJV:

Obey them that have the rule over you, and submit yourselves; for they watch for your souls, as they must give account, that they may do it with joy, and not with grief: for that is unprofitable to you.

In order to grow, we need to understand the BIG PICTURE. That is what Paul is saying. What is it that GOD IS SEEKING TO ACCOMPLISH ? Anything that bucks against the order that God has established must be dealt a death blow, appealable only by genuine repentance.

There are other instances of divisions in the Word to let us know not to be caught off guard by, and how to handle, them. Moses and Aaron, his brother and assistant, had their moments of strife, especially over Moses' wife and the molten gold calf that Aaron claimed 'jumped' out of the fire.

Orpha left Ruth and Naomi to fend for themselves after promising to pull together on one accord.

Joseph's brethren sold him to marauders because of a dream. They were cruel enough to dip his coat of many colors in blood to convince their aged father that his beloved son was dead.

The spies were sent out together, but only Joshua and Caleb came back with a 'we are well able...' good report. They saw the same thing but were subject to different influences. Environment colors perception which can, in turn, engender strife.

Cain and Abel came from the same womb, but jealousy caused one to murder the other and address God with a conscience seared with a hot iron: 'Am I my brother's keeper?'

Esau and Jacob had a blood lust fueled by the divisiveness and the secretive preferential treatment of their own mother, Rebekah!

These kinds of rife battles riddle the Bible, but we are to have the same care one for another. Love is to be without dissimulation or hypocrisy. Romans 12:9; Galatians 2:13 KJV. If the battle is not subdued, the body will devour itself. According to Malachi 3 KJV, we must 'rebuke the devourer'! Paul saw the end from the beginning. What a conflagration a little fire kindleth. James 3:5 KJV

That strife is part of the strain of the growth process is evident in Paul's letter to the Ephesians, as well, where he warns the saints to walk worthy of the vocation wherewith they are called, with ALL *lowliness and meekness,* each ESTEEMING THE OTHER better than themselves, longsuffering and forbearing one another in love. That's quite the diet and requires considerable mastication before swallowing. It is meat. The fighting is milk.

Proverbs 20:3 KJV:

It is an honor for a man to cease from strife, but every fool will be meddling.

This proverb is the first cousin to blessed are the peacemakers…

Ephesians 4:3-6 KJV clarifies 'the beseeching' of Euodia and Syntyche by Paul and the walk expected of saints:

Endeavoring to keep the unity of the Spirit in the bond of peace.

There is one body and one Spirit even as ye are called in one hope of your calling.

One Lord, One faith, One baptism, One God and Father of all, Who is above all and through all and in you all.

ALL or nothing is his premise. Every now and then we have to return to the first landmark as the stark reminder: DENY YOURSELF, DAILY TAKE UP YOUR CROSS AND FOLLOW ME.

As aforementioned, Euodia and Syntyche were not the only squabblers. We learn from our own mistakes. Paul was not exempt from the same 'vices'. There was quite the infamous battle over whether John Mark should accompany them on another missionary journey.

Ministering, recognizing our own imperfections, is sobering and lends itself to compassion, to say the least.

CHAPTER 8

KOINONIA: UNIFIED ON THE MOUNT OF GOD

We must keep our eyes on the prize, Paul would say, not only to Euodia, Syntyche, and his other understudies, but to this generation as well.

Love will cause us to look at one another as sisters.

Love will stop us from letting unwholesome words proceed out of our mouths but only that which is godly and edifying.

Love will cause us to esteem the other women better than ourselves.

Love will cause us to pull together rather than apart recognizing that a threefold cord (us, them, and Christ) is not easily broken.

Love will cause us to stop before walking in the counsel of the ungodly, standing in the way with sinners and sitting in the seat of the scornful.

Love will cause us to look below the surface for the cause of the scowl or perceived bitterness and standoffishness of another sister to see what undisclosed pain may be brewing there that needs to be healed.

For Euodia and Syntyche to be warring roses while Paul is calling them beloved is to **speak into them** what God intends, not what is actually happening or how they are currently behaving. Stop! That will preach right here! Glorrrrry! Whatever the outward appearance, God tries the heart because He always remembers that what is beneath the visible mess in us is an invisible and holy God---Christ in us the hope of glory.

Never lose sight of the fact that the directive to love comes from on High. IT IS THE BOND OF PERFECTION.

Bond infers *'koinonia'. Koinonia* is fellowship, sharing, a collection, communion, joint participation---intimacy either with God or one another or both. Love is the glue that keeps us in place (I Corinthians 12, 14 KJV). LOVE does not vaunt or parade itself, is not puffed up, does not behave itself unseemly, does not seek its own but the other person's good, is patient, is kind, does not take into account a wrong suffered (I Corinthians 13 KJV).

Love comes from the Chief EXECUTIVE, COMMANDER IN CHIEF, THE ONLY TRUE GOD WHO IS SEATED ON THE MOUNT OF THE CONGREGATION (ISAIAH 2:2; 14 KJV), THE SIDES OF THE NORTH, the first mountain of the eight (Psalms 30 KJV):

We MUST get it together and level the playing feel with understanding, compassion, and love if we expect to get in the HOUSE.

The Word that Isaiah the son of Amoz saw concerning Judah and Jerusalem:

Micah 4:1-4 KJV

And it shall come in the last days that the mountain of the Lord's House shall be established in the top of the mountains, and shall be exalted above the hills, and all of the nations shall flow unto it.

And many nations shall come and say come let us go up to the mountain of the Lord, and to the house of the God of Jacob; and He will teach us of His ways and we will walk in His paths; for the law shall go forth of Zion, and the word of the Lord from Jerusalem.

And He shall judge among many people, and rebuke strong nations afar off, and they shall beat their swords into plowshares and their spears into pruninghooks; nation shall not lift up a sword against a nation, neither shall they learn war any more.

But they shall sit every man under his vine and under his fig tree, and none shall make them afraid: for the mouth of the Lord hath spoken it.

There shall come a time when all shall flow to the Mount of God. God is love. AS SUCH, UNLIKE SOME, GOD IS NOT GOING TO ALLOW ANYTHING AND EVERYTHING IN HIS HOUSE. 'ON EARTH AS IT IS IN HEAVEN' DOES NOT INCLUDE THE JUNK IN THE TRUNK.

We must put down the weapons that we war with, especially our tongues. We ain't gonna study war no more. Abba has spoken. We will put down the carnal weapons, the swords, and spears. They will be transformed from weapons of destruction into implements of peaceful coexistence and nurturance.

The weapons of our warfare are not carnal but mighty through God to the tearing down of strongholds (2 Corinthians 10:4 KJV).

God's heart's desire is that we prosper and be in health even as our souls prosper. The only way to achieve this is through unity and unity requires that we love.

From the world's perspective, it seems impractical and impossible in this day and age to lecture about love. Yet, it was love that brought us to it and it is love that will help us do it.

Proverbs 20:3 KJV:

It is an honor for a man to cease from strife, but every fool will be meddling.

This proverb is that the first cousin to blessed are the peacemakers…

Matthew 5:44-45 KJV:

Love your enemies, Bless them that curse you, do good to them that hate you, and pray for them which despitefully use you, and persecute you; that ye may be the children of your Father which is in heaven for He maketh His sun to rise on the evil and on the good, and sendeth rain on the just and unjust.

The depiction of God's Mountain portrays just that. No more fighting. No more war. The wicked will cease from troubling, as the songwriter states, and the weary will be at rest.

Our ultimate goal is Psalms 133 KJV: Behold how good and pleasant it is for brethren to dwell together in unity.

Psalm 133 is in a group of Psalms called the ascents. In entering the tabernacle there were 14 steps (Psalm 120 -134 KJV) which is the number of each of the three groups of Jesus' genealogy 14 x 3 in Matthew 1 KJV. The ascents refer back to Micah 4:1-4: 'Come let us go UP to the mount of the Lord.'

The three reflects the three major Jewish feasts, ***shalosh regalim,*** when they went up to worship God (***Yeshua Hamashiach***) of

Abraham, Isaac and Jacob (three again). The three major feasts were Passover (**Pesach**), Pentecost (**Shavuot**), and Tabernacles (**Sukkot**). On each step or ascent, the priests would sing one of the aforementioned Psalms.

The feasts kept the people bonded together. Community is the fulfillment of the word *unity*. The kind of strife and disagreement that we see in Euodia and Syntyche, Hymaneus, Hermogenes, Alexander, and Philetus is set aside for the greater good.

There can be greater works reflective of greater love by laying aside one's life for one's friends. Further, united under Christ, we are a royal priesthood, a holy nation, a peculiar people destined to declare His praises (I Peter 2:9 KJV).

God has called us to peace. That peace is bred by the Holy Spirit, the Ruach that was breathed upon us in Genesis at creation was lost or buried in sin. God reinvested in us by Christ who prayed to the Father to send the Comforter, the Paraclete, the one alongside, who will lead and guide us into all truth. We are whole again.

Paul is calling Euodia and Syntyche back to the source---GOD!

GOD is Love…

CLOSING PRAYER

If there is an issue, if there is a bone of contention, a dispute, the resolution of it lies in the Word of God says Paul. He says I am a true representative because I follow in the footsteps of Christ and urge you, Euodia and Syntyche, to do likewise.

I Corinthians 1:6 KJV-

Howbeit we speak wisdom among them that are perfect; yet not the wisdom of this world, nor of the princes of the world, that come to naught:

But we speak the wisdom of God in a mystery, even the hidden wisdom, which God ordained before the world unto our glory.

Which none of the princes of this world knew for had they known, they would not have crucified the Lord of Glory.

But as it is written, Eye hath not seen, nor ear heard, neither hath entered into the heart of man, the things which God hath prepared for them that love Him.

But God hath revealed them unto us by His Spirit; for the Spirit searcheth all things, yea the deep things of God.

What God has prepared is inextricably, invariably intertwined with His Only Begotten Son, the Firstborn from the dead who 'they that worship, must worship Him in Spirit and in truth.'

MY PRAYER IS THAT WE HOLD FAST OUR PROFESSION OF FAITH, NOTHING WAVERING, STEADFAST UNTO THE END:

Romans 8:35-39 KJV:

WHO SHALL separate US FROM THE LOVE OF CHRIST? SHALL TRIBULATION OR DISTRESS, OR PERSECUTION, OR FAMINE OR NAKEDNESS OR PERIL OR SWORD?

AS IT IS WRITTEN, FOR THY SAKE WE ARE KILLED ALL THE DAY LONG; WE ARE ACCOUNTED AS SHEEP FOR THE SLAUGHTER.

NAY IN ALL THESE THINGS WE ARE MORE THAN CONQUERORS THROUGH HIM THAT LOVED US.

FOR I AM PERSUADED THAT NEITHER DEATH, NOR LIFE, NOR ANGELS, NOR PRINCIPALITIES, NOR POWERS, NOR THINGS PRESENT, NOR THINGS TO COME.

NOR HEIGHT, NOR DEPTH, NOR ANY OTHER CREATURE, SHALL BE ABLE TO SEPARATE US FROM THE LOVE OF GOD WHICH IS IN CHRIST JESUS OUR LORD.

AND IT IS INDEED IN THAT NAME THAT IS ABOVE EVERY OTHER, THE NAME OF THE ANOINTED ONE, CHRIST JESUS, THAT WE PRAY THIS PRAYER. AMEN.

INSPIRATIONAL BIBLIOGRAPHY

1. Nelson's NKJV The New Open Bible Thomas Nelson Edition
2. Max Lucado, The Devotional Bible NCV
3. Nelson's New Illustrated Bible Commentary
4. The Chumash, The Stone Edition, Mesorah Publications
5. Exegeses Parallel Bible
6. The New Strong's Exhaustive Concordance of the Bible
7. Dake's Annotated Bible
8. The Expositor's Study Bible
9. Halley's Bible Handbook
10. Matthew Henry's Multivolume Commentary of the Bible
11. The Interpreter's Bible
12. The Bethany Parallel Commentary of the Old Testament
13. The Bethany Parallel Commentary of the New Testament
14. The Oxford Companion to the Bible
15. Wilson's Dictionary of Bible Types
16. A Dictionary of Scripture Proper Names by J.B. Jackson
17. The New Compact Bible Dictionary by Zondervan
18. The Companion Bible
19. The Greek English Lexicon of the New testament and other Early Literature by Walter Bauer
20. New Gospel Parallels Volumes I and II

21. The Hebrew-Greek Key Study Bible (KJV Baker) Spiro Zodiates
22. Number in Scripture by E.W. Bullinger
23. The Pulpit Commentary
24. The Eerdmann Atlas of the Bible
25. The Expositor's Study Bible by Jimmy Swaggart
26. The Spiritual Warfare Bible
27. The Message Bible
28. Bartlett's Familiar Quotations

OTHER BOOKS BY THE AUTHOR

CASTAWAY CRADLES Amazon (Oct. 2014) e-book Bestselling author in counselling, religion & social issues

JUNIA ARISE, APOSTOLIC WOMEN ON THE FRONTLINES Alpha PUBLISHING (2018) CONTRIBUTING AUTHOR WITH APOSTLE AXEL SIPPACH

CRUMB SNATCHERS XLIBRIS (2014) ISBN 978-1-4931-2189-2 978-1-4931-2190-8

BE XLIBRIS (2014) ISBN 978-1-4931-2832-7 978-1-4931-2833-4

GOD, GRACE & GRIT XLIBRIS(2014) ISBN 978-1-4990-6130-7 978-1-4990-6129-1

FOOTSOLDIERS XLIBRIS (2014) isbn 978-1-4990-1931-5 978-1-4990-1930-8

POMEGRANATE PERFECTION, TOPICAL SERMON COMPILATION AUTHORHOUSE (2013) ISBN 978-1-4772-8251-9 978-1-4772-8258-8

CHRIST: THE PREEMINENT THRONE AUTHORHOUSE (2012) ISBN 978-1-4685-4928-7 978-1-4685-4927-0

SEEK YE FIRST THE KINGDOM Rosedog (2012) ISBN 978-1-4349-8516-3 978-1-4349-7510-2

KINGDOM SEED XLIBRIS (2011) isbn978-1-4653-8171-2 978-1-4653-8172-9

ACCEPTED IN THE BELOVED XLIBRIS (2011) ISBN 978-1-4653-0708-8 978-1-4653-0709-5

CAKE, CRUMBS & CRUSTS, AN ANTHOLOGY OF SERMONS RED LEAD PRESS (2012) ISBN 978-1-4349-6634-6 978-1-4349-2611-1

THREE C'S FOR THE SEASONED TRIAL LAWYER (2012) 978-1-4349-6673-5 978-1-4349-2650-0

ECHOES OF UNREQUITED LOVE by Cynthia Kay King. Red Lead. press (2012) isbn 978-1-4349-6585-1 978-1-4349-2562-6 ; Dr. MizCyn King Authorhouse (2014) isbn 978-1-4918-5842-4 isbn 978-1-4918-5841-7

ABOUT THE AUTHOR

Apostle Dr. Cynthia King Bolden Gardner is a dedicated advocate in law and in the body of Christ. Born premature in 1955 and immediately declared as good as dead, she immersed herself in her Beloved Abba, Adonai Jehovah, as early as 18 months graced Prophetic dreams and visions.

She is accustomed to the Pauline brand adversity that accompanies effectual and great open doors. She has known strife, division and the ragged edge from birth. Fast forward 63 years, she is an accomplished scribe of 21 books in the past decade plus one bestseller in Christian Counseling, Social Issues and Religion.

Apostle Gardner readily identifies with Euodia and Junia having grown up and practiced in male dominated legal ministerial professions with women as her staunch antaagonists.

Her passion is public speaking, writing, inventing and battling community and domestic violence, while mediating and drafting initiatives against police brutality.

She is a celebrated semi-retired government and private sector attorney. The courtroom and pulpit are both arenas to propound righteousness and deliverance.

Graduating from Georgetown Schools of Foreign Service,1978 and Law, 1981, Dr. Gardner is licensed in Ohio, California and Pennsylvania. She has founded 3 churches and presently serves as Presiding Bishop of New Mercy Seat Ministries, International, an EPIC Global Tier I Leader, Bishop and Legal Adviser for NRFOCC. Her lifelong pursuits are youth advocate and mentor, Champion of the homeless, disadvantaged, addicted and disenfranchised. At home she enjoys relaxing with her children which are 7 GERMAN Shepherds, 4 horses and a bull.

www.ingramcontent.com/pod-product-compliance
Lightning Source LLC
Chambersburg PA
CBHW051708090426
42736CB00013B/2604